THE CAREGIVING CRISIS

WHAT IT COSTS YOUR BUSINESS AND HOW TO FIX IT

BY DEBBIE HOWARD

Ritz Books
STORIES THAT CHANGE THE WORLD

The Caregiving Crisis:
What It Costs Your Business and How to Fix It

Copyright © 2021 Debbie Howard
ISBN: 979-8-9856592-0-7

Published by RITZ BOOKS
A Division of Steph Ritz LLC

RitzBooks.com
STORIES THAT CHANGE THE WORLD
A SMALL YET RESPECTABLE VANITY PRESS PUBLISHING HOUSE
FOR VISIONARY LEADERS AND SPIRITUAL ENTREPRENEURS

Ritz Book guides authors to create books, courses, stage talks, websites, marketing, and educational materials for professional development, self-improvement, healing, and online learning. We support entrepreneurs, business professionals, and industry leaders to voice their passions. Do you have a book idea, or have you already written a book manuscript you'd like us to consider publishing? Please visit www.RitzBooks.com to learn more.

DEDICATION

I dedicate this book to companies of all sizes
working to better support employee wellbeing
across the full spectrum of life's stages,
including the wellbeing of those employees
who care for aging loved ones.

ABOUT THE AUTHOR

Debbie is a former caregiver on a mission to change the way the world looks at caregiving so the impacts are not so devastating for companies and their employees who are also tasked with caregiving responsibilities at home. To that end, her work focuses on providing companies with the support they need to mitigate the growing risks with employee turnover, low productivity, and future healthcare costs.

Prior to founding Aging Matters International (AMI) and The Caregiving Journey in 2016, Debbie lived and worked in Japan for 30 years, where she founded and built a market research consultancy and continues to translate consumer research into clear strategic direction for Fortune 500 global clients across a wide range of categories, including age-tech.

During her time there, Debbie also served as President and Chairman of the American Chamber of Commerce in Japan (ACCJ) from 2004~2007 and as President Emeritus (2008~present), advocating for regulatory reforms to help international businesses succeed in Japan.

With the launch of AMI, Debbie created a conduit for both amplifying caregiver-related challenges and providing solutions to address those challenges, combining her personal caregiving experience with her market research and corporate communications acumen.

Her latest book, *The Caregiving Crisis: What It Costs Your Business and How to Fix It*, provides company leaders with guidance and a clear way forward for managing productivity and retention challenges, including practical ways to create more caregiver-friendly workplaces.

In addition to drawing on Debbie's 40-some years in business and her personal experience as a live-in caregiver for her mom, her recommendations are enriched by interviews with more than 100 business leaders, managers, employees, and service providers.

Debbie's first book (*The Caregiving Journey: Information. Guidance. Inspiration.*) helps individuals choose their best way forward in guiding family members and loved ones to the end of their lives with love, ease, and grace.

Map out a clear pathway forward to save money and build corporate goodwill while supporting your caregiver employees with strategic planning for the future, targeted content, and educational training programs.

Learn more at www.TheCaregivingCrisis.com

Table of Contents

FOREWORD

Long before COVID, there was another global healthcare crisis brewing – the caregiving crisis.

Caused by the convergence of two macro trends in our world – rapid aging and over-burdened healthcare systems – the caregiving crisis impacts both individuals and the companies they work for.

I'm talking about family caregiving – a job in which unpaid and primarily untrained family members take on the responsibility of caring for aging loved ones, often at the risk of their own health and wellness.

These employees represent right at 30% of every company's workforce, and they're spending an average of 24 hours per week as a caregiver in addition to their full-time employment with you.

The full cost to companies of the caregiving crisis is difficult to calculate. At its core it includes employee turnover, absentee-ism, and future healthcare costs. Official estimates are 68 billion dollars annually for US companies today. These costs are expected to more than double over the next 20 years or so.

The prolonged pandemic has shined a glaring spotlight on the negative impacts of at-home care responsibilities on caregivers' emotional, physical and financial health. Moreover, it has stimulated discussion about the sheer viability of working at all under such stressful conditions. Perhaps most importantly, the pandemic has intensified the imperative for companies to find new ways of supporting caregiving employee needs, whether related to adult caregiving or child caregiving.

Women are disproportionately responsible for handling the caregiving roles in our society, so it's not surprising that more women than men have been forced to leave the workforce during the pandemic.

However, even before the pandemic, employees caring for aging loved ones represented at least one-fifth of the workforce. Perhaps more importantly, they were also becoming increasingly diverse. For example, Millennial-aged caregivers of adults aged 50 or over topped 10 million in the summer of 2019. Meanwhile, male caregivers represent a rising percentage of all caregivers, increasing from 35% to 39% since 2015.

Supporting working caregivers therefore sits solidly at the intersection of human capital management, DEI (diversity, equity, and inclusion), and employee experience. Taking it one step further, as a business in the communities where you operate, by assuming a leadership role through Corporate Social Responsibility (CSR) activities and community outreach, you'll be contributing to building healthier and more productive communities overall.

The Caregiving Crisis: What It Costs Your Business and How to Fix It details the challenges of our global caregiving crisis and outlines practical and cost-efficient solutions for you and your company to use in proactively addressing the needs of this expanding and increasingly diverse segment of your workforce.

CAVEAT: I'd like to state right now that my mom taught me to stay out of discussions about politics – and I've always found that has worked fairly well for me. With this in mind, I pledge to do my best to report on The Caregiving Crisis – and what companies can do about it – in an unbiased manner.

PART 1:

THE UPFRONT ANSWERS YOU NEED, RIGHT UP FRONT

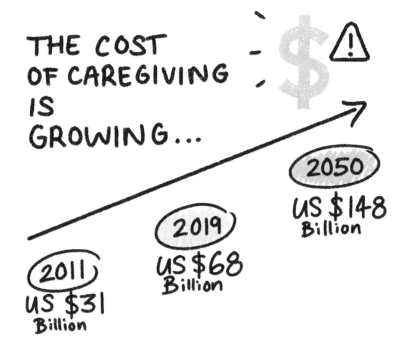

US COMPANIES LOSE $68 BILLION ANNUALLY IN CAREGIVER-RELATED COSTS

The annual costs related to aging caregiving alone have more than doubled since 2011, from $31 billion to $68 billion in 2019. More escalation is in sight, with costs estimated to again more than double to $148 billion annually by 2050.

There is mounting evidence to demonstrate the business case for implementing caregiver-friendly policies. For starters, it saves you money by:

- *Reducing healthcare costs for your company*

- *Improving retention of valuable employees (and their expertise!) so they can continue with their work for you when their caregiving is done*

- *Enhancing the productivity of caregiving employees while they're caregiving*

- *Attracting new talent going forward*

- *Contributing to the fulfillment of overall employee experience, DEI, and human capital management initiatives*

And there's more good news – it turns out that it's quite EASY and cost-efficient to support your caregiver employees.

There are a number of companies actively working to address the needs of employee caregivers. However, unfortunately, supports that go beyond what is mandated by law are only available at about one-third of all companies. The bar is low for making a big difference in YOUR company.

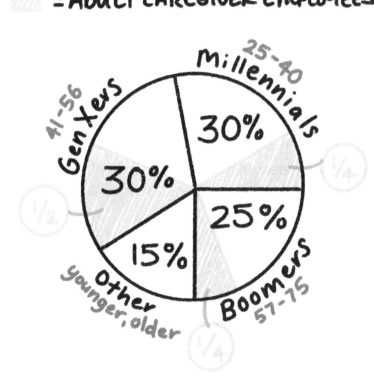

YOUR WORKFORCE

= ADULT CAREGIVER EMPLOYEES

ONE-THIRD OF ALL EMPLOYEES CARE FOR AGING LOVED ONES IN THEIR NON-WORK HOURS… AT AN AVERAGE OF 24 HOURS PER WEEK

The prolonged pandemic has shined a spotlight on just how devastating the duty of care can be, cutting across all age groups, genders, ethnicities, and pay grades, regardless of whether work is remote or not.

- *Caregivers of aging parents and spouses/partners aged 50+ already represented 20-25% of your workforce before the pandemic. The pandemic created many new caregivers of adults, raising this number to 30%.*

- *Millennial-aged employees represent one-quarter of all caregivers of adults aged 50 and over. Perhaps the hardest hit are those GenX and Millennial caregivers who are doing double duty as so-called "sandwich caregivers" – caring for both aging parents while still raising children at home. While women have been disproportionately affected, it's important to keep in mind that 40% of all caregivers of adults aged 50 and over these days are men.*

- *The prolonged pandemic also expanded the definition of caregivers to include parents of normal children, who were suddenly thrust into the world of home schooling.*

The caregiving crisis is playing out in companies, communities, and countries all over the world, as family caregivers of all age groups and genders struggle to support their loved ones with aging and moving to the ends of their lives.

THE BURNING QUESTION: DOES YOUR COMPANY HAVE A SOLID PLAN FOR MANAGING THE CAREGIVING CRISIS?

To get started with planning, some of the key questions to ask are:

- *Do you know who your caregiver employees are?*

- *Are you and your managers trained in how to engage your employee caregivers (and those at high risk) – so you can provide the support they need during this difficult period in their lives?*

- *What types of policies do you have in place to manage hybrid working situations (i.e., work-from-home/remote working versus in-office working)?*

- *What Human Resources (HR) programs do you already have in place? (i.e., overall health and wellness, self-care, financial preparedness, and specific-to-caregiving care coordination, grief management, and life re-orientation post-caregiving)?*

- *What is the caregiving crisis costing your business?*

Developing a solid plan about how to manage the needs of this special employee segment is pretty straightforward. *The Caregiving Crisis: What It Costs Your Business and How to Fix It* will tell you how, step-by-step.

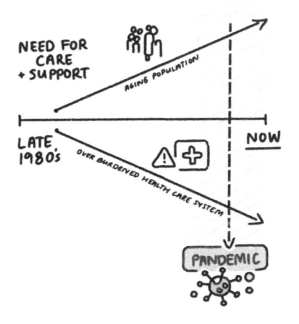

NEED FOR
CARE
+ SUPPORT

AGING POPULATION

LATE
1980's

NOW

OVER BURDENED HEALTH CARE SYSTEM

PANDEMIC

WORLDWIDE:

[1 BILLION AGED 65+]

10% POPULATION WW
30% JAPAN
20% ITALY
15% S. KOREA
20% EUROPE/EU

FOR EVERY
PERSON
AGED 65+
→

THERE IS
AT LEAST
1x FAMILY
CAREGIVER

THE CAREGIVING CRISIS HAS BEEN A LONG TIME IN THE MAKING; IT'S NOT GOING AWAY

Consider that:

- *With 10,000 people turning 65 every day in the US, the number of older adults is set to nearly double from some 54 million today to 90+ million in 2050.*

- *Government and social safety nets are strained.*

- *As a result, half of those aged in their 40s and 50s right now – and many of those aged in their 20s and 30s – will be called on to help support aging loved ones in the next five years.*

- *Companies are stepping in because many caregivers also work full-time, and the negative impacts of the duty of care have become so evident.*

- *As a result, risk mitigation related to employee retention, productivity, and healthcare cost management is becoming a prevalent discussion topic – even in the Boardroom.*

- *The caregiving crisis is global – driven by the same trends as in the US of rapid population aging in combination with an increase in chronic conditions and over-burdened healthcare systems.*

- *The caregiving crisis has been gaining momentum for some 30 years, and will heighten in ferocity moving forward.*

There can be no doubt that however urgent the imperative is today to support employee caregivers, it will only become more pressing moving forward.

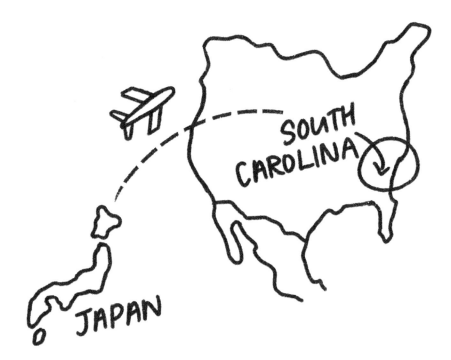

PERSONAL WORK, PERSONAL IMPACTS ... MY STORY

I know firsthand about the utter chaos families face when there is a sudden caregiving need.

- *Without warning, my Mom was diagnosed with Stage 4 Lung Cancer. She was an active and healthy 74-year-old with a family history of living into her late 80s.*

- *After only one year of light support, both of my two sisters' paid time off via the Family Medical Leave Act (FMLA) was exhausted.*

- *For her final six months, the only option was for me to leave Tokyo (where I'd been living and running my business for over 20 years) and return to South Carolina – where I'd grown up – to serve as her live-in caregiver.*

- *I ran my Tokyo-based business from Mom's dining room table, including leveraging my mobile laptop-lifestyle and hybrid working skills, relying on my non-caregiving team members back in Japan, and gaming time zones while Mom slept.*

- *I'm not going to tell you it was easy… but our situation was SO MUCH BETTER than for most because: A) We had a plan long before Mom needed help. B) She had long-term healthcare insurance (LTHC). And C) We were able to get hospice care.*

But even with this best-case scenario – and without the pressures of Covid – my sisters and I suffered: physically, emotionally, and financially.

That's because like many of your employees, we stepped up to personally fill the gap that current healthcare systems simply do not address, with hospitals and rehabilitation centers pushing ever more complex medical treatments onto untrained family members.

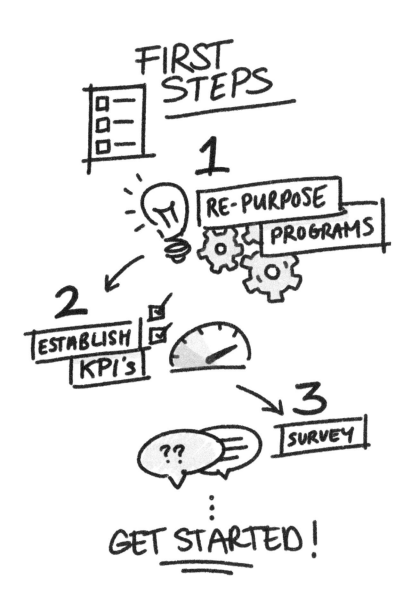

SO WHAT ARE YOUR FIRST STEPS IN ADDRESSING THE CAREGIVING CRISIS IN YOUR COMPANY?

Three actions you can take immediately are:

- *Review existing EAP and other programs, and re-purpose selected programs (i.e., for overall health and wellbeing, working Moms and parents, for financial readiness, etc.) with a life stage view, to include meeting the specific needs of caregivers.*

- *Establish Key Performance Indicators (KPIs) in harmony with other HR-related KPIs to benchmark and monitor employee caregiver-related progress and risk assessment going forward.*

- *Survey your employees to identify who your working caregivers currently are (as well as those at high risk for burnout, preferred means of support, awareness of company offerings, anticipated caregiver responsibilities, etc.). For managers, utilize regular meetings and/or more formalized surveys to discuss manager challenges and needs related to employee caregivers.*

The solutions are not complicated or costly. But it does require that you get started, sooner rather than later.

WHAT OTHER PRACTICAL SOLUTIONS MAKE SENSE?

Armed with greater knowledge about your employee caregivers, clear KPIs, and a plan for repurposing and existing programs, you are ready to further proactively manage the negative impacts of the caregiving crisis on your business. Beyond these first three easy actions, the solutions roadmap is rich, including:

- *Adding programs to address gaps in your caregiver support ecosystem.*

- *Acknowledging your caregiving employees by featuring their stories in employee publications, recognizing their efforts while encouraging preparedness and improving awareness of available programs.*

- *Utilizing your employee caregiver support programs for greater positive impact across your stakeholder universe: managers, employees, current and customers, suppliers, legislators… and in the communities where your business operates.*

There are many ways to move forward with meeting the needs of your employee caregivers, starting with leadership and creating a virtuous cycle that encompasses training and skills building, coaching and resources, and relevant content.

Because company cultures vary so greatly, each company must find its own unique way forward. In *The Caregiving Crisis: What It Costs Your Business and How to Fix It*, I guide you through your options.

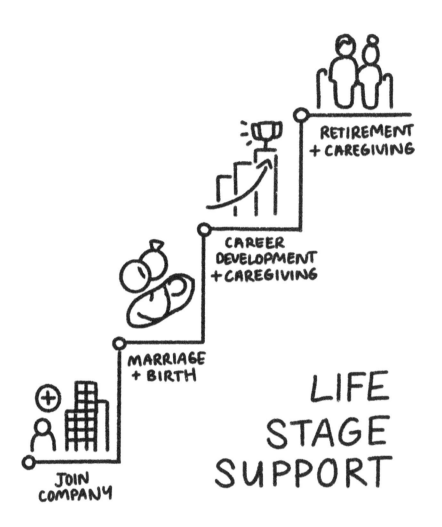

EMPLOYEE WELLBEING AND EXPERIENCE ENHANCE RETENTION AND IMPROVE PRODUCTIVITY

The idea of companies enhancing productivity through support of their employees' healthy and balanced lifestyles has gained tremendous momentum during the prolonged pandemic.

As part of fostering employee wellbeing, life stage needs are increasingly taken into account – including the caregiving scenarios that naturally occur for young children through to aging parents.

With caring for employee caregivers at the intersection of human management, DEI, and employee experience, companies today have an extraordinary opportunity.

I encourage you to consider the implications of including life stage needs as a natural aspect of your company's initiatives to improve workplace support and experience for ALL employee types.

Not only are there obvious productivity benefits to employee wellbeing; creating a caregiver-friendly workplace also gives companies a competitive advantage for talent acquisition.

Considering the devastating impact of the caregiving crisis on employees and companies, supporting the substantial segment of employees who care for aging loved ones just makes good business sense.

Check out the wealth of resources for addressing the caregiving-related costs at your company at www.TheCaregivingCrisis.com

Here, you will find:

- Programs assessment and repurposing worksheet
- KPI worksheet
- Employee survey "how to's" and key questions
- Thoughts on leveraging employee touchpoints

... and MORE!

Or better yet, bring me in to help you fast track mapping out a forward-thinking strategy for a more caregiver-friendly workplace – a strategy based on your unique company culture.

Whether you already have a few programs in place or you're just getting started, I can help your company build a strong foundation that leverages the positive impacts with all your stakeholders, starting with your employees.

Reach out to me to start a discussion today:

www.TheCaregivingCrisis.com/Contact

https://www.linkedin.com/in/debbiehoward/
https://twitter.com/debbiethecarer/
https://www.instagram.com/debbie.howard.5264/

PART 2:

FIXING

THE BROKEN SYSTEM

FOR

EMPLOYEE CAREGIVERS

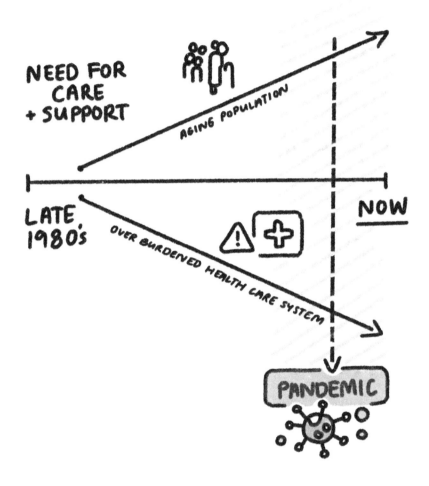

A GLOBAL CHALLENGE
THAT IS NOT GOING AWAY

The phenomenon of the caregiving crisis is complex and is magnified by several key factors:

- *Rapid aging worldwide*
  - ~ *By 2030, there will be at least 300 million more people aged 65+ compared to 2014.*
  - ~ *This means there is also a higher number of aging caregivers, some with health conditions of their own (i.e., average caregiver age is 49 in the US; in Japan, it's 65).*
  - ~ *It also creates more diversity in caregiver ages, with younger family members increasingly required to help.*
- *Greater need for support with IADLs and ADLs*
  - ~ *Longevity is great, but there is also a cost as more support is typically needed for managing daily life activities as people age.*
  - ~ *Rising incidence of chronic health conditions (heart, diabetes, dementia and Alzheimer's, even cancer) among aging populations is also expanding the need for support.*

IADLs and ADLs are the standardized evaluation criteria used by the medical profession and the insurance industry to determine access to compensation.

Instrumental Activities of Daily Living (IADLs)
and Activities of Daily Living (ADLs)

The first level of needs is called Instrumental Activities of Daily Living (IADLs) and refers to activities not considered necessary for fundamental functioning, but which nonetheless allow someone to live independently.

- Cooking
- Driving
- Using the phone or computer
- Shopping
- Paying bills
- Managing medications

The next level of needs is more critical to living on one's own, and is referred to as the six Activities of Daily Living (ADLs).

- Eating
- Bathing
- Dressing
- Toileting
- Transferring/walking
- Continence

Further magnification of the caregiving crisis results from the following factors.

- *More people on brink of financial solvency as they move into their final years*
  - ~ *The dramatic effect of expanded care needs and skyrocketing healthcare expenses means increased numbers of those outliving their money.*
  - ~ *In the US, the problem is exacerbated among those aged 65+ by lack of retirement preparedness as well as low incidence of long-term healthcare insurance (LTHC) coverage (7% of those aged 50+).*
- *More expensive healthcare costs*
  - ~ *Rising healthcare costs have become a global reality as governments, companies, and institutions in the medical, healthcare, and other caregiving-related industries struggle with delivery of services.*
- *Scarcity of paid healthcare professionals*
  - ~ *Even before COVID, demand exceeded supply, and there was a shortage of qualified care professionals (i.e., nurses, CNA's, home health aides, etc.).*
  - ~ *Continued and expanding pressure on healthcare-related and medical-related institutions leaves fewer resources available for paid in-home support.*

IN 2015, THE WORLD HEALTH ORGANIZATION (WHO) WARNED THAT HEALTH SYSTEMS AROUND THE WORLD ARE FALLING SHORT WITH MEETING THE NEEDS OF OLDER PERSONS.

This observation can be extended to apply to those caregivers who provide unpaid care for elderly care receivers as well.

WORLDWIDE:

[1 BILLION AGED 65+]

- 10% POPULATION WW
- 30% JAPAN
- 20% ITALY
- 15% S. KOREA
- 20% EUROPE/EU

FOR EVERY PERSON AGED 65+ → THERE IS AT LEAST 1 x FAMILY CAREGIVER

My own awareness of the challenges presented by an aging society comes largely from the fact that I've lived and worked in Japan for over 30 years.

IF YOU HAVEN'T ALREADY HEARD, JAPAN IS
BY FAR THE MOST RAPIDLY AGING COUNTRY
ON THE PLANET, WITH 30% OF ITS POPULATION
AGED 65 OR MORE RIGHT NOW;
OF THOSE, ONE-THIRD ARE AGED 80+.

I wrote about it in my regular column for the Nikkei Weekly, way back in 2008:

"The demographic tidal wave that has made Japan the most aged society in the world is already straining social systems, including pensions and healthcare. It represents a foundational shift affecting the nation's overall economic and social fabric, and has also placed Japan center stage as other countries watch carefully to see how Japan grapples with the phenomenon."

It turns out that although rapid population aging is most accelerated in Japan, this phenomenon is also occurring in virtually all developed countries worldwide:

- *European countries follow closely after Japan (with Italy next in line), struggling with 20-23% of their populations aged 65+ (and around one-third of these seniors aged 80+). In the UK and Canada, the comparable number is 17%.*

- *In the US, Australia and New Zealand, the aging challenge is also notable – with roughly 15% of these populations aged 65 or older right now, and one-quarter of these seniors aged over 80.*

- *The same aging trend can also be seen in other Asian countries, such as South Korea, China and Thailand, which are gaining quickly.*

By the year 2050, each of the above-mentioned countries will have anywhere from 25% to 40% of their populations aged 65+.

> ALONG WITH THIS GLOBAL TREND OF AGING, THERE COMES A TREMENDOUS COST TO THE EVER-GROWING NUMBER OF THOSE INDIVIDUALS WHO WILL NEED CARE – AND A TREMENDOUS COST TO THOSE INDIVIDUALS WHO WILL BE CALLED UPON TO GIVE CARE.

Globally, there are nearly one million family caregivers right now providing close to one trillion dollars per year in free caregiving services, valuing their time at minimum wage.

To put that in perspective, even five years ago, US caregivers provided an estimated value of US$470 billion in unpaid care (again, if their time were valued at minimum wage), which is three-quarters of the annual Medicare budget.

> BY THE YEAR 2050, THERE WILL BE NEARLY 2 BILLION PEOPLE AGED 65+ WHICH WILL NATURALLY INCREASE THE NUMBER OF CAREGIVERS NEEDED TO SUPPORT THEM.

The impact starts first with the individual, placing pressure on physical, emotional and financial conditions. It then naturally ripples outward to include negative impacts on companies, governments, and society at large.

MEANWHILE, RIGHT HERE IN THE US-OF-A

In the US alone – which is the predominant focus of *The Caregiving Crisis: What It Costs Your Business and How to Fix It* – the triple whammy of "rapidly aging population" + "increasing chronic care needs" + "over-burdened healthcare system" has created a very frightening situation.

Based on the latest available statistics (April 2020) from AARP and the National Alliance for Caregiving, there has been a rapid increase in the number of caregivers in the US from 2015 to 2020, with at least 53 million Americans now serving as unpaid caregivers to an adult or child with special needs.

That's one in five adults, and the number is rising in keeping with aging demographics in the US, with 10,000 baby boomers turning 65 every day.

Caregiving in the U.S.
Based on Age of Care-Receiver

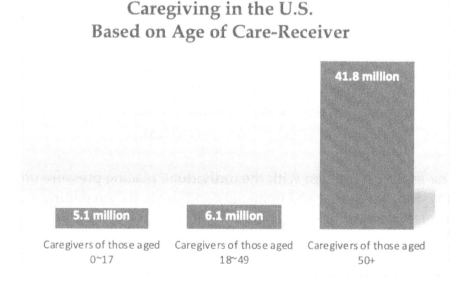

		41.8 million
5.1 million	6.1 million	
Caregivers of those aged 0~17	Caregivers of those aged 18~49	Caregivers of those aged 50+

Source: 2020 Report: Caregiving in the U.S., AARP and NAC

The report projects that by 2050, the U.S. population of older adults will have nearly doubled to 83.7 million people.

> CONSIDERING THE DATA COLLECTED OVER
> THE PAST 20 YEARS, THERE IS NO DOUBT THAT
> THE NUMBERS OF THOSE BEING CARED FOR
> ARE DEFINITELY ON THE RISE.

The AARP study also showed that over half of American caregivers feel they had no choice as to whether to help or not, and that they are:

- *More likely to be caring for more than one person now (24%, up from 18% in 2015).*

- *Having greater difficulty coordinating care (26%, up from 19%).*

- *Caring for someone with Alzheimer's disease or dementia (26%, up from 22%).*

- *Feeling the pressure, with more family caregivers saying caregiving has made their own health worse (23%, up from 17%).*

- *Representing multiple generations, including not only Boomers, but also GenX, Millennials – and even those at younger ages.*

The caregiving crisis is here now

Because three-quarters of all caregivers of adults aged 50 and over ALSO work full-time, the domino effect of negative impacts in the workplace has become evident.

WHAT DOES ALL THIS MEAN FOR COMPANIES?

For companies, the caregiving crisis is creating:

- *Challenges with turnover (one-third of caregivers leave their jobs because they just cannot handle all that's required of them at work and at home)*

- *A feeling among employee caregivers of not being supported – which contributes to even higher resignation rates*

- *A drain on institutional knowledge*

- *Issues with reduced productivity (absentee-ism and presentee-ism <being at work, but in a very preoccupied state due to the not fully being there mentally due to concerns with caregiving>)*

- *Escalated future healthcare costs, due to the devastating negative effects on caregivers–emotional, physical, and even financial– that reverberate long after caregiving is done*

From a positive viewpoint, there is mounting evidence to show that even providing simple caregiver supports pays off.

STUDIES SHOW THAT FOR EVERY US$1.00 INVESTED IN FLEXTIME AND TELE-WORKING, BUSINESSES CAN EXPECT A RETURN RANGING FROM US$1.74 TO US$4.34.

Another piece of good news is that addressing employee caregiver needs doesn't have to be expensive. Many existing programs for other employee segments can be re-purposed to fit their needs (i.e., programs for working Moms, for emotional wellbeing, even for financial planning).

When considering retention and talent acquisition, having a caregiver-friendly workplace is a benefit that is increasingly sought after by GenX and Millennial employees and candidates and is factored in when recognizing "Best Places to Work."

THE IMPACT OF CAREGIVING WILL BECOME
MORE PRONOUNCED… AMERICA'S EMPLOYERS
WILL NEED TO REDUCE INSTANCES IN WHICH
WORKERS ULTIMATELY LEAVE THE WORKFORCE
AS A CONSEQUENCE OF CAREGIVING
OBLIGATIONS, AS WELL AS ELIMINATE BARRIERS
TO WORKFORCE PARTICIPATION AND REENTRY.
CURRENTLY, THE CHOICE TO LEAVE
OR REMAIN OUT OF THE WORKFORCE
OFTEN HINGES ON THE ABILITY OF EMPLOYEES
TO BALANCE THEIR ROLES AT WORK
AND RESPONSIBILITIES AS CAREGIVERS.
THAT WILL NEED TO CHANGE.

Source: The Caring Company, Harvard Business School, 2019

Helping you to view your employee caregivers as a distinct employee sub-segment is a core competency at AMI, and it's a good first step toward exploring employee caregivers needs, which in turn helps to mitigate the related cost impacts of turnover, absentee-ism, and escalated healthcare costs.

Contact me for a free 30-minute consultation to discuss how your company can identify and better understand the needs of your employee caregivers.
www.TheCaregivingCrisis.com/Contact

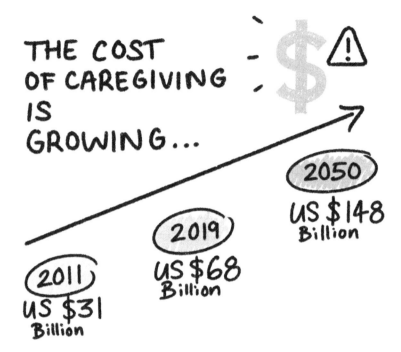

THE COST OF CAREGIVING IS GROWING...

2011
US $31 Billion

2019
US $68 Billion

2050
US $148 Billion

WHAT ABOUT THE COSTS?

The hidden costs related to caregiving in the workplace are estimated to be 68 billion dollars annually right now and are expected to more than double over the next 20 years or so.

There are obvious costs related to the short-term effects of absentee-ism and presentee-ism. But perhaps even more costly for companies is the cost to replace and retrain the one-third of employee caregivers who must ultimately leave their jobs because their caregiving responsibilities at home have simply become too overwhelming.

> FOR A WHITE-COLLAR WORKER WITH A US$80,000 ANNUAL SALARY, THE COST TO REPLACE AND RETRAIN IS US$160,000… FOR A BLUE-COLLAR WORKER WITH A US$60,000 ANNUAL SALARY, THE COST TO REPLACE AND RETRAIN IS US$120,000.

In addition, there are longer-term increases in healthcare costs due to the negative impacts on employee emotional and physical health, which in turn also create an ongoing negative spiral for future generations to deal with.

Yet because the majority of companies don't track costs specifically related to caregiving, it's been difficult for most to gain a firm grasp of exactly how much the caregiving crisis is costing them.

One of the important topics covered in my deep dive strategy planning sessions is the establishment of KPIs that fit within your current company ecosystem to help you establish benchmarks for caregiving-related costs, and to monitor them going forward.

Let's talk about establishing a few key KPIs that will work for your company. Contact me at www.TheCaregivingCrisis.com/Contact

In Addition to the Costs to Your Company, the Negative Financial Impacts on Your Employees are Also Worth Noting

Out-of-pocket Expenses

Caregivers reportedly spend over $7,200 per year in out-of-pocket expenses (for medicine, groceries, healthcare, travel expenses, and housing maintenance) on behalf of their loved one. Facility expenses (i.e., assisted living or nursing facility fees), are additional (average US$5,000 per month; for memory care US$7,000 per month).

Lost Wages

In addition, many caregivers end up leaving the workforce early to focus on providing care. Analysis by MetLife (from a report in 2016) calculated the resulting lost wages at US$324,000 for women and US$283,000 for men.

Depleted Savings, Unpaid Bills, etc.

With the average time of providing care at 4.5 years (and 5+ years for one-third of all caregivers), many suffer from eroded savings accounts. One-quarter use up their short-term savings completely, and 15% must borrow money from family or friends to make ends meet.

Worse yet, as with the negative impacts on emotional and physical health, these negative financial impacts in turn also create financial problems for the caregiver in THEIR retirement, and the negative spiral for future generations continues.

At the broader economic level, the Economist Intelligence Unit and AARP calculated in their 2020 report (The Economic Impact of Supporting Working Family Caregivers) that if employed family caregivers age 50-plus have access to workplace support, US GDP could grow by an additional $1.7 trillion by 2030 and by $4.1 trillion (or 6.6%) in 2050.

The report further projected that even using the most conservative outlook (i.e., one in which the number of those engaged in family caregiving does not expand), the economic impacts would still be significant, and importantly, if family caregivers aged under 50 were factored in, the economic impacts would be much larger.

THE CAREGIVING CRISIS: A STORM BREWING FOR QUITE SOME TIME

You might be surprised to learn that the caregiving crisis has been identified and discussed for well over 30 years now. There has been much excellent work done in terms of supporting working and non-working caregivers, including that done by early adopter companies. Evidence supporting the business case for caregiver-friendly workplace policies is growing.

However, the challenges are so large, multi-faceted, and deeply pervasive (yet at the same time somehow hidden) in society and workplaces, it's taken a global pandemic of epic proportions and duration to escalate awareness of and attention to the issues.

As Ellen Galinsky, President of the Family Work Institute (FWI) and co-author of FWI's 2016 National Study of Employers said in 2017:

> *"I remember we said that eldercare was going to be the benefit of the 90s because the population was aging. Then we said it was going to be the benefit of the 2000s… and (next) the 2010's."*

As a market researcher and analyst, I've found it fascinating to research the caregiving crisis, along with its impacts on companies, over the past 15 years.

Much informative work has been conducted before and during this time by government, academia and business consortiums.

You can find links to access these reports in the References section near the end of *The Caregiving Crisis: What It Costs Your Business and How to Fix It*, and on our website: www.TheCaregivingCrisis.com

Research has shown strong agreement for these three statements, regardless of who sponsored the studies:

1. The cost of addressing employee caregiver needs doesn't have to cost a bundle.

2. Many existing programs for other employee segments can be re-purposed to fit the needs of employee caregivers (i.e., programs for working moms, for those struggling with emotional challenges, etc.).

3. Some of the most highly-valued supports from the viewpoint of employee caregivers are flex time and paid time off.

Today, about one-third of all companies have more than what is legally mandated in place to support their employee caregivers. For many more companies, the pressures of the pandemic are encouraging active exploration into overall workplace experience, including support for employee caregivers (where it is not currently being provided).

While early corporate attention has primarily gone to supporting parent caregivers, progressive organizations are implementing support programs designed with a life stage viewpoint, which includes addressing the needs of all types of caregivers.

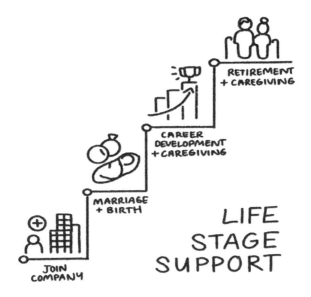

The idea of bringing a life stage viewpoint to all HR and EAP offerings goes beyond the idea of employee engagement based on their employment journey, taking into account important "life transitions" such as caregiving responsibilities – whether those are for younger children or aging loved ones.

> EMPLOYERS HAVE LONG SUPPORTED
> MATERNITY AND, MORE RECENTLY
> PATERNITY LEAVE RELATED TO CHILDBIRTH,
> A CELEBRATORY TIME. FOR PARENTS WITH
> GROWING CHILDREN, EMPLOYERS HAVE
> SUPPORTED TIME AWAY FOR CHILDHOOD
> ILLNESS, BALL GAMES, MUSIC RECITALS, ETC.

Creating a life stage culture that supports employee caregivers throughout their caregiving and work careers – and acknowledges the gift these employees are providing to their families – is gaining greater acknowledgement as good business practice.

PART 3:

A CRISIS

FOR COMPANIES

AND THEIR

EMPLOYEE CAREGIVERS

A MANDATORY SECOND JOB – READY OR NOT!

Your employees are also family members who are increasingly called upon to serve as the caregivers for their aging loved ones in the absence of adequate help and support from their communities, state and national government, and society-at-large.

Your employee caregivers:

- *Spend an average of 24 hours per week on their caregiver responsibilities (in addition to their full-time work)*

- *Are largely untrained for the task at hand, yet are increasingly required to perform complicated medical procedures at home, as the range and volume of care responsibilities pushed onto family caregivers expands*

- *Struggle with the negative emotional and physical impacts of their additional care responsibilities; many will also suffer from financial strain and stress*

Each caregiving situation is as unique as the individuals involved. The duration of caregiving time as well as the depth and breadth of caregiving needs can vary greatly.

Many factors contribute to the level of difficulty in a given caregiving situation, including:

- *Care receiver - physical, emotional, cognitive, and financial health*

- *Caregiver - physical, emotional, and financial health*

- *Living circumstances of care receiver (living alone, with spouse/grown child, in assisted living/nursing facility, etc.)*

- *Presence (or absence) of siblings, and when there are siblings, level of cooperation among them*

- *Whether your employee is the primary caregiver, versus playing a support role as a secondary caregiver*

- *Whether caregiving is "emergency-driven" (or not)*

- *Whether the family has discussed caregiving and what planning is in place, however minimal*

Aside from the above variables, two over-arching drivers typically draw the initial boundaries around the logistics for a given caregiving situation:

- *Aging support scenario of the care receiver*

- *Physical proximity between the caregiver and the care receiver*

Three aging support scenarios ...

There are three main aging scenarios related to the natural progression of aging under normal and unexpected circumstances. The level of support required by employee caregivers is determined by their care receiver's level of mobility, mental clarity, and ability to live independently.

Three Broad Scenarios in Aging and Approaching the End of Life

1) Age naturally with either:

   - *Minimum of health-related challenges; ability to safely live independently*

   - *Combination of health-related issues that restrict performance of IADLs or ADLs (making independent living impossible)*

2) Age with diagnosis of <u>short-term disease</u> (e.g., cancer, leukemia, stroke) that restricts performance of IADLs/ADLs over a <u>shorter-than-average</u> caregiving period (4.5 years or less).

3) Age with diagnosis of <u>longer-term</u> disease (e.g., memory loss, dementia, Alzheimer's, Parkinson's, ALS, pulmonary fibrosis) that restricts performance of IADLs/ADLs over a <u>longer-than-average</u> caregiving period (4.5 years or more).

Source: The Caregiving Journey: Information. Guidance. Inspiration. 2018

Age naturally with limited health challenges

In this scenario, the care receiver's overall physical and cognitive brain health and mobility are stable with very few challenges, and independent living is viable pretty much until the end of life.

THERE IS SLOW BUT STEADY DETERIORATION
RELATED TO AGING, WITH SMALL EXPECTED
MEDICAL CHALLENGES RELATED TO THE
NATURAL AGING PROCESS (E.G., CATARACTS,
KNEE OR HIP REPLACEMENTS, DIABETES,
PACEMAKER), BUT NOTHING TOO DRAMATIC OR
INSURMOUNTABLE IN TERMS OF ALTERING
LIFESTYLE.

Minimal support may be required at first, but as time goes by, more support will no doubt be needed with driving, running errands, meal preparation, and other daily activities.

The loved one is able to age and die at home (or perhaps in assisted living or hospice), mainly due to natural causes and largely without much medical intervention or prolonging of life by artificial means.

Age naturally with combination of health challenges that hasten inability to live independently

In this scenario, the aging care receiver's health condition and mobility become so compromised that independent living is no longer an option.

SPECIFICALLY, HEALTH STARTS
DETERIORATING, WITH A SERIES OF SMALL
MEDICAL CHALLENGES; THEN THERE IS A FALL,
A STROKE (OR WORSENING OF AN EXISTING
CONDITION SUCH AS HEART DISEASE OR
DIABETES) THAT RESULTS IN RESTRICTION OF
IADLs AND ONWARD TO ADLs.

Depending upon the severity of the situation, much help and support can be required, either sporadically or continuously. However, it sooner rather than later becomes clear that living independently is no longer possible or will not be viable for long.

Final days, months, or years might be spent at home or in an assisted living facility. But most likely, support from medically trained professionals will be required to meet the care receiver's daily needs.

Diagnosis of short-term or long-term disease

With a more specific disease diagnosis, such as cancer or Alzheimer's, there is typically a natural course or outcome that can be projected from a medical perspective.

FOR GOOD OR FOR BAD,
A SPECIFIC DISEASE DIAGNOSIS CAN
REQUIRE A DIFFERENT EMOTIONAL MINDSET
FOR THE CAREGIVER
COMPARED WITH CAREGIVING
RELATED TO THE NATURAL AGING PROCESS.

Differences in mindset are particularly notable when thinking about a short-term prognosis of 1.5 years for cancer versus a longer-term prognosis of 8~10 years for Alzheimer's.

Proximity also contributes to intensity of caregiving

After considering specific health conditions, proximity is the next most important driver in determining caregiving roles and responsibilities.

TYPICALLY, ONE PERSON IN A FAMILY WILL
ULTIMATELY FULFILL THE ROLE OF "PRIMARY
CAREGIVER"; IT'S USUALLY THE PERSON WHO
CAN SPEND THE MOST CONCENTRATED TIME
WITH THE CARE RECEIVER.

However, in most families, it takes contributions from several members to support a loved one adequately. Unless a person is completely disengaged from the situation (and therefore uninvolved in caregiving for the care receiver), there are two main possible roles.

Up Close and Personal

The primary caregiver typically lives with or in close proximity (within one hour) to the loved one. It could be 24/7 (living in the loved one's home, or with them living in your home), or it could be living near their assisted or nursing facility.

From Afar

This caregiver lives farther away, needing at least several hours to physically "get to" the loved one. Daily access is not possible. With the more far-flung geographic nature of modern families, the advent of the From Afar caregiver is more prevalent than several generations ago and is rife with its own stressors.

ONE-THIRD OF EVERY COMPANY WORKFORCE, AND GROWING

Statistics related to the universe of your caregiving employees have been an upwardly moving target since the beginning of the pandemic. However, even before COVID, the number of those employees caring for aging loved ones was a hard 20%.

That percentage has expanded to at least 30% with the pandemic, with many employees:

- *Finding their "light" caregiving responsibilities increase for aging loved ones who previously lived independently with little or no support.*

- *Feeling entirely new levels of stress when their loved ones' facilities were/are locked down – prohibiting visits and check-ins with facility staff.*

- *Bringing aging loved ones home to live with them (from assisted living and nursing centers), in the interest of safety. Most say they will continue with at-home caregiving, creating expanded caregiver responsibilities for the long-term.*

- *Becoming so-called sandwich caregivers (tasked with caring for their parents while still raising children).*

- *Suffering from the negative impacts of the duty of care, with both emotional and physical health problems emerging.*

Considering the macro forces of rapid population aging, increasing incidence of chronic conditions, and over-burdened healthcare systems, there is no doubt the number of your employees who care for aging loved ones will steadily increase in the coming years.

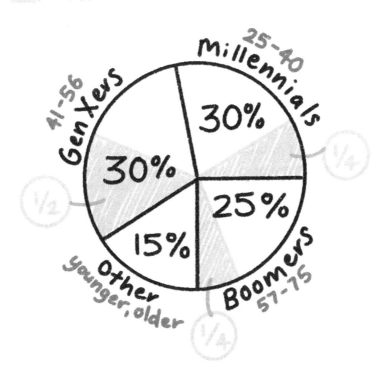

YOUR WORKFORCE

= ADULT CAREGIVER EMPLOYEES

Millennials 25-40 — 30%

GenXers 41-56 — 30%

Boomers 57-75 — 25%

Other younger, older — 15%

1/4 1/2 1/4

EMPLOYEE CAREGIVERS: A DIVERSE AND AT RISK EMPLOYEE SEGMENT

Aside from representing 30% of every workforce, there are several characteristics about caregivers of aging loved ones that make them an important employee segment:

1. There is a universality in the way that aging caregiving responsibilities alight upon employees of all ages, ethnicities, genders, and pay grades. When loved ones need help, they need help.

2. There are now many younger caregivers (one-quarter are Millennial-aged), as well as male caregivers… and perhaps the hardest hit of all, sandwich caregivers. The stereotypical image of caregivers as "49-year-old females" is a dangerously misleading image.

3. The negative impacts on caregivers' emotional, physical, and financial health are well documented.

In short, caregiving impacts a naturally diverse group in very similar ways.

Age-wise, approximately half of all family caregivers are under the age of 50, with many of these younger employee caregivers taking on caregiving duties for adult family members while still raising their own children.

Among employee caregivers, the prevalence is slightly higher for caregivers with "low" and "medium" burdens, with "high intensity" burden caregivers less well represented.

This is because one-third of caregivers end up leaving their jobs due to overwhelming prolonged caregiving situations, or as the end of their care receivers' lives approach.

In the early days of caregiving, an employee might need to request only a few hours off here and there, for such responsibilities as taking a loved one to a doctor's appointment. If the caregiver lives in the same town as the loved one, that may not be so unmanageable. But what if the caregiver lives several states away, and there is no one else to help out?

Over time, as the care receiver's need for support grows and help with daily living activities is required, your working employee will no doubt become seriously overloaded with family obligations to the point that (in pre-COVID times) they're not able to physically be in the office eight hours a day.

IN MANY CASES, EMPLOYEES SUFFER
FROM HEALTH PROBLEMS OF THEIR OWN
DUE TO THEIR INCREASED LEVEL OF STRESS,
WHICH AFFECTS THEIR PERFORMANCE
BOTH AT WORK AND AS A CAREGIVER.

The sad fact, again, is that one-third of all employee caregivers ultimately quit their jobs, sometimes at the height of their careers, in order to care for their aging parent or spouse. Careers that were humming along just fine are sidetracked – and even ended forever – because these employees' caregiving duties become so onerous there is no other option.

Another sad fact is that as many as one-third of all caregivers also suffer financial ruin due to their caregiving responsibilities – creating waves of poverty for aging generations of the future.

There is no doubt that economics come into play when caregiving help is needed.

WITH AN AVERAGE OF $7,000 PER MONTH
FOR MEMORY CARE IN ASSISTED LIVING,
AND $20.00 PER HOUR
FOR UNSKILLED HOME CARE HELP,
THE COSTS BECOME
UNAFFORDABLE VERY QUICKLY.

Having financial resources can help ease the pain… but no matter what, the caregiving situation is rather devastating on a number of levels, even in the best of cases. Even WITH resources, there is such a shortage in the home help and caregiving industries it's become very challenging to find reliable support for in-home aging in place, or otherwise.

I KNOW… IT HAPPENED TO ME!

I'd like to tell you a little bit about my story. I had been living and working in Japan for a little more than 20 years when I learned my mother had less than two years to live. It threw my life and my family's lives into an uproar.

By this time I was dividing my working time between Japan and the US, and was on a much-needed break at my home in beautiful Central Texas.

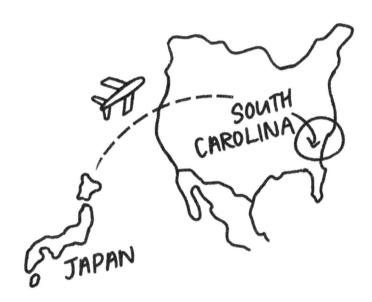

When I got "the call" I was 53, lounging in bed on a brilliant, sunny morning in May. I had just completed a very intense three-year stretch of Japan-based work and I was looking forward to finally having some time to myself. I was happily thinking "THIS will be 'the summer of Debbie.'" My mind was abuzz with plans for gardening, closet cleaning, and a spa trip to focus on learning Pilates.

I could see the red flash of cardinals flitting from tree to tree, and I could hear the low, intermittent thrum of the hummingbirds at the feeders. I awoke slowly and luxuriously, feeling like I had all the time in the world.

Little did I know that with that one phone call, everything would change in a nanosecond.

As I advise in my first book (*The Caregiving Journey: Information. Guidance. Inspiration.*), one of the most important preventive actions every individual can take is to have a plan for how caregiving will be handled, well before there is an emergency situation.

In our case, we were so lucky to have discussed and planned many of the details related to Mom's end-of-life wishes long before she was diagnosed with cancer. This made it much easier for us to move quickly and work together to make the most of the situation.

We sorted out the final details of her will, along with legalities and financial details related to real estate and personal property disbursement, including naming of Power of Attorney and estate executor, and we knew that she wanted to be cremated.

We also had time to visit with family friends and to take a few trips to visit favorite spots of ours from over the years.

While we weren't wealthy by any means, we were reasonably solvent. My mom worked her heart out as a single Mom raising three teenaged girls in the '70s - working her way up from an executive secretarial position to a purchasing manager position for a Fortune 500 company. She'd managed to support us AND save enough for her retirement. She did without to make sure she wouldn't be a burden on us, and she had a goal to age in place and die at home, if at all possible.

My sisters and I were all self-sufficient, with promising careers in the private sector, healthcare, and government. We all, including Mom, owned our own homes.

Yet nothing could have prepared any of us for the emotional devastation of losing Mom and the wake of financial pressures that followed. Having a plan well in advance gave us a fighting chance – but it still took everything we had!

Please refer your employees to our complimentary "20-Point Planning Checklist" under Resources at www.TheCaregivingJourney.com

In addition to your employees having a solid plan for how they will handle caregiving for their loved ones, other important considerations include how close they live to their care receiver and how well they get along with and are able to coordinate with their siblings (if they're lucky enough to have them).

Here too, we were fortunate. During the first year following Mom's diagnosis, I increased the frequency of my trips back and forth between Tokyo and Greenville, South Carolina (where I grew up). My two sisters – one who lived nearby and the other who lived three states away – and I took turns spotting each other to make sure we had good coverage in terms of supporting Mom.

Thank goodness there were three of us, and we all got along and were able to manage it fairly smoothly. But the last six months of Mom's life were an entirely different story.

Once it became clear that Mom could no longer make it on her own without help, I shifted quickly from being a secondary caregiver From Afar to being a primary caregiver Up Close and Personal. That's because after only one year, both of my sisters' FMLA benefits were exhausted. Because I had my own business, I was the only one able to go live with Mom to provide 24/7 support.

So I left my young team in Tokyo handling daily operations and moved back to South Carolina, running my Tokyo-based business from the dining-room table where we'd all eaten together since my elementary school days.

We managed to get through it, though as with most caregiving situations, it was very traumatic.

As it was, my 1.5 years of caregiving (during which I was unable to focus exclusively on my business) placed me in a weakened position in terms of the post-caregiving period.

NO ONE COULD HAVE PREDICTED
THE GLOBAL FINANCIAL MELTDOWN OF 2008.
LATE THAT YEAR IS WHEN MOM PASSED AWAY.
BECAUSE OF THIS PARTICULAR TIMING,
I WENT INTO THE PERIOD
JUST FOLLOWING MY MOM'S PASSING
IN A VERY COMPROMISED STATE –
IN MORE WAYS THAN JUST FINANCIAL.

As the world descended into global financial turmoil, especially in Japan, I struggled to save the shreds of my business, all while grieving.

Like so many caregivers, I and my sisters were depleted emotionally and physically from our caregiving and work responsibilities. We were worried about our own financial futures, too.

In the years since I served as Mom's caregiver, I've reexamined my motivations in life at large and the deeper meaning of all that happened during that time when Mom was dying.

We did the best we could as a family under the circumstances, and we did a good job. We all worked together to grant Mom's wish to die at home – and believe me, it took everything we had.

> CONTRIBUTIONS OF INFORMAL CAREGIVERS
> GO UNNOTICED, EXCEPT BY THOSE
> WHO BENEFIT FROM THEIR CARE.
> HOWEVER, IT'S IMPORTANT
> TO RECOGNIZE THAT THE CONTRIBUTIONS OF
> INFORMAL CAREGIVERS ARE IRREPLACEABLE.
> NO SOCIETY, RICH OR DEVELOPED,
> CAN AFFORD TO REPLACE
> ALL INFORMAL CAREGIVERS WITH
> PAID, PROFESSIONAL HEALTHCARE WORKERS.

Sometimes I can't help but wonder: How much more could we have made of our final days together? This is one of the driving forces behind my involvement in the aging and caregiving arenas.

HYBRID WORKING: PROS AND CONS

There is no doubt the pandemic pushed the boundaries for all caregivers, increasing both the time required and the pressures related to caregiving.

The hybrid working conditions that have been instituted for all employees (both work-from-home and remote working versus in-office working) are not new territory for most caregivers. In fact, caregivers could be called the original hybrid workers.

WORKING AT HOME UNDER DURESS IS
WHAT CAREGIVERS NATURALLY DO.
NEW BOUNDARIES MUST BE SET
SO THAT BOTH WORK AND CAREGIVING
CAN CO-EXIST.

The officially sanctioned nature of hybrid working has for some caregivers been a relief. But at the same time, it has added a layer of stress because there is no physical escape or change of pace afforded from having to go to work (or being able to go to work.)

MANY CAREGIVERS FIND A RELEASE IN THE
NORMALCY OF THE WORK ENVIRONMENT
COMPARED TO THEIR
HOME CAREGIVING ENVIRONMENT.

On the other hand, returning to work also becomes more complicated for caregivers with vulnerable older loved ones now living with them, heightening concern about return-to-work due to the greater COVID exposure risk involved.

EMPLOYEE CAREGIVERS: YOUR HARDEST-PRESSED (AND OFTEN HIDDEN) EMPLOYEES

It's also important to note that many caregivers don't think of themselves as caregivers per se.

One of the reasons for this is related to the continuum of caregiving. In the early stages of caregiving, for example, responsibilities may be limited to accompanying the care receiver on doctors' visits once in a while. Many don't identify such early support activities as caregiving.

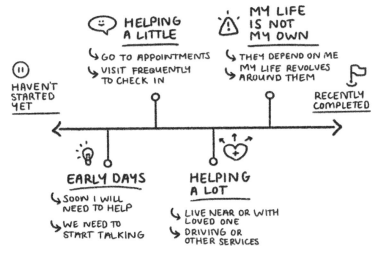

SOURCE: THE CAREGIVING JOURNEY: INFORMATION. GUIDANCE. INSPIRATION. 2018

Culture also comes into play; specifically, attitudes toward caregiving can vary depending on ethnicity. For example, in Asian cultures, caring for one's aging loved ones is typically more expected as a natural part of the life experience and therefore might not be as likely to be acknowledged as "caregiving."

Another reason is the sometimes-negative stigma attached to caregiving for aging loved ones. Many employee caregivers downplay or even hide the fact they're serving as caregivers. They worry about asking for the support they need because they fear being looked over for promotions, being fired, or not even being hired in the first place.

> JUST SLIGHTLY OVER HALF OF
> EMPLOYED CAREGIVERS REPORT
> THAT THEIR SUPERVISOR IS AWARE
> OF THEIR CAREGIVING RESPONSIBILITIES.

One telling fact is that among the reasons given for use of FMLA in one survey, "caregiving for an adult family member" is way down at the bottom of the list. Conversely, more socially palatable reasons top the list, such as caring for a sick child or recovering from an injury.

Perhaps it's because there's an unwritten, unspoken expectation that one should somehow have had a better plan in place. That's usually not possible, though, because most caregiving situations happen quite unexpectedly: diagnosis of Alzheimer's at an early age, or stroke resulting in paralysis, or an adult child being stricken with spinal meningitis. It's pretty impossible to plan for the unthinkable.

One additional underlying reason for the stigma is that unlike caring for children – which is generally viewed as a happy, hopeful activity that society recognizes and embraces (and does not view as a burden) – caring for the aging has a different feeling to it. This is another reason why looking at employee needs from a life stage viewpoint is important.

THESE CIRCUMSTANCES ALL
CONTRIBUTE TO UNDER-REPORTING
WHEN IT COMES TO CONFIRMING
INCIDENCE OF EMPLOYEE CAREGIVERS –
OVERALL AND WITHIN SPECIFIC COMPANIES.

Yet the evidence is clear – the impact of the duty of care, wherever an employee may be on the caregiving continuum – is disruptive to work and productivity, and sadly, often leads to the employee leaving the workforce altogether.

Work-related Challenges of Employee Caregivers:

- *33% have unplanned absences*
- *28% have late arrivals at work*
- *17% have early departures from work*
- *54% feel their assignments are not challenging*
- *50% of caregivers get lower salary increases or bonuses*
- *46% are unsatisfied with their career path*
- *80% admit to lower productivity*
- *32% have left a job*

Source: AARP and NAC: Caregiving in the US 2020

Defining Caregivers and Caregiving – Not as Simple as You Might Think

One of the challenges in the landscape of caregiving is the word "CAREGIVER" itself.

Indeed, I personally did not even know the word "caregiver" while I was caregiving for Mom. Yet now I know the term caregiver has been widely used to refer to non-professional, unpaid family caregivers of adults aged 50+ since at least 1995.

Still, when I'm speaking with someone new to the term, their first association is "professional" caregiver – i.e., nurse, certified nursing assistant, or other medically-trained professional working in a hospital, rehabilitation center, or in-home care agency. Professional caregivers can work full- or part-time, via an employer or independently. There are also those who work as volunteers.

> THAT'S WHY I'M ALWAYS CAREFUL TO DEFINE
> THE TYPE OF CAREGIVER I'M TALKING ABOUT
> BY SAYING: "UNPAID, NON-PROFESSIONAL,
> FAMILY CAREGIVER" (WHAT A MOUTHFUL).

Even once that distinction is made, there's a further disconnect with "caregiver type." Research studies recognize three main types of family caregivers, all of which are said to "care for an adult or child with special needs."

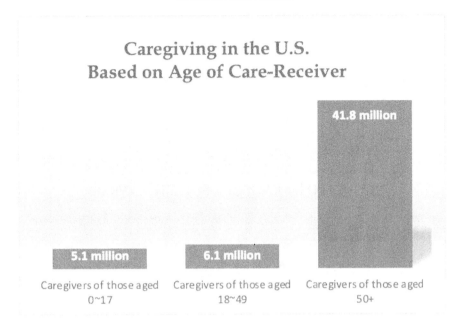

Caregiving in the U.S.
Based on Age of Care-Receiver

41.8 million

5.1 million

6.1 million

Caregivers of those aged 0~17

Caregivers of those aged 18~49

Caregivers of those aged 50+

Source: 2020 Report: Caregiving in the U.S., AARP and NAC

Next, there is the caregiving role itself – is it primary, or is it a secondary role on the caregiving team? A secondary caregiver can be another family member, or a trusted friend or relation who can be relied upon for support.

Are parents of normal children "caregivers?"

Strictly speaking, no, since the definition of caregiver implies that the care receiver is somehow sick or disabled.

THE PANDEMIC GREATLY HEIGHTENED
AWARENESS OF THE CHALLENGES
OF CONSTANT CARE
WHEN CHILDREN WERE RESTRICTED
TO HOME ENVIRONMENTS.

The resulting and overwhelming duty of care caused mass departures of women from the workplace (3 million women and counting). Even worse, recovery of female workforce participation to pre-COVID levels is expected to lag two years behind that of males.

> THE SHEER MAGNITUDE OF THE DUTY OF CARE ACROSS GENERATIONS HAS NATURALLY RESULTED IN A WIDER USE OF THE TERM.

Carers, caretakers

To confuse the situation even further, the term caregiver is not used worldwide. Specifically, the term "carer" is commonly used in British English.

There's also the term "caretaker," which I don't like because technically it refers to someone who cares for something that isn't a person, whether in American or British English.

Final thoughts on terminology

Another topic is aging- related terminology. You will hear various terms related to aging and caregiving, including:

- Eldercare
- Senior care
- Aging care

In defining "the caregiving crisis" at Aging Matters International (AMI), the primary focus is supporting those caring for aging loved ones, since the crisis largely results from the phenomenon of rapid aging. I personally have a strong preference for the term "aging care" since many who are aging do not appreciate being referred to as "elderly" (eldercare)... or as "seniors" (senior care).

A GLOBAL CHALLENGE WITH VERY INDIVIDUALIZED IMPLICATIONS

With 1 billion people right now aged 65+ globally (a number that will double by the year 2050), the need for aging care support is growing exponentially.

Yet only about 5% of families have had the deep and heartfelt discussions required to address aging care in a fully thought-out manner. For most families it takes a sudden event (i.e., a fall, a disease diagnosis, even a pandemic) to force serious conversations – and what will actually be required through the end of life.

As a leader, you've heard about it. You may have felt it personally. You've seen your employees struggling with their caregiving responsibilities. You know your company is feeling the negative impacts of the slow yet steady drain on profits.

For perspective, over half of those you know will be tasked with caregiving responsibilities within the next five years.

The impact starts first with the individual, influencing their physical, emotional and financial condition. It then naturally ripples outward to impact companies, governments, and society at large.

Statistically speaking, even without the pandemic you (and those you know, including your employees) are at high risk of serving as a caregiver sooner rather than later. It already happened to me.

PART 4:

WORKPLACE SOLUTIONS ROADMAP

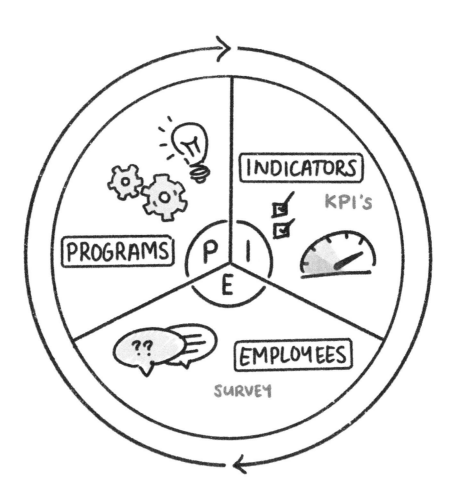

GETTING STARTED IS AS EASY AS "P-I-E"

Improving your company's support for employee caregivers definitely takes a bit of thought, intention, and attention. But it doesn't have to be complicated.

ALONG WITH THE WORLD'S TRANSFORMATION
INTO A SO-CALLED GIG ECONOMY AND
THE ADVENT OF THE PANDEMIC,
THE TRANSFORMATION OF WORKPLACES
IS ALREADY UNDERWAY.

By getting started now – either from scratch or by enhancing supports you already have in place – you'll be minimizing the negative impacts of the caregiving crisis on both your company and on your employee caregivers.

I've outlined three important actions you can take on the following page.

The solutions are not complicated or costly. But it does require you to get started, and the sooner you start, the better it will be for your company and your employee caregivers.

I'll be happy to lead you and your team through a deep dive workshop where together we'll surface the best way forward for your unique company needs. Contact me for a free 30-minute consultation:
www.TheCaregivingCrisis.com/contact

1. PROGRAMS: Review existing EAP and other programs and re-purpose selected programs (i.e., for overall health and wellbeing, for working Moms and parents, for financial readiness, etc.) with a life stage view in order to meet the specific needs of caregivers. Draft out a provisional plan for expanding the supports currently offered.

2. INDICATORS: Establish KPIs in harmony with other HR-related KPIs to benchmark and monitor employee caregiver-related progress as well as to assess risk going forward.

3. EMPLOYEES: Survey your employees to identify who your employee caregivers currently are, including their risk for burnout, awareness of company offerings, preferred means of support, anticipated caregiver responsibilities, etc.). For managers, utilize regular meetings and/or more formalized surveys to discuss manager challenges and needs related to employee caregivers.

PROGRAMS:
REVIEW CURRENT OFFERINGS AND IDENTIFY WHICH PROGRAMS CAN BE RE-PURPOSED

Many companies have benefits portfolios offering employees a range of insurance, retirement, paid time off, paid medical leave, flexible scheduling, education assistance, and more.

Those with the most generous benefits packages offer further access to a wider range of products, such as insurance, financial and/or wellness counseling, and online identity theft protection.

Looking at what your company already offers and repurposing selected programs for the specific needs of employee caregivers where possible is a logical first step.

Review, identify and re-purpose

The first and easiest targets in terms of re-purposing existing programs to the more specific needs of employee caregivers are:

- *Health and wellness programs that maintain and improve future health conditions.*

- *Coaching and counseling programs for stress management and burnout avoidance (or any off-work problem affecting productivity).*

- *Financial planning and retirement planning programs that help mitigate future financial risks.*

- *Any flexible time or remote/hybrid working programs.*

- *Any 'working Mom' or 'working parent' programs related to maternity, paternity, or otherwise having an allowance of paid or unpaid time off for the purpose of providing care to their children while their jobs are held open for them.*

These program areas are all natural pathways for adding modules that drill down on information that is specific to caregiving and caregivers.

> REGARDLESS OF WHETHER THESE BENEFITS ARE
> OFFERED AS "INCLUDED" OR "VOLUNTARY,"
> THE SAME BENEFITS SHOULD BE AVAILABLE TO
> THOSE WITH AGING CARE RESPONSIBILITIES,
> WITHOUT FEAR OF STIGMATIZATION.

Three consistent results from multiple studies serve as a great starting point for all companies in terms of ensuring HR policies and programs meet the growing needs of your employee caregivers:

- *Time and flexibility are what employee caregivers value most of all, indicating strong appreciation of generous leave policies that are both unpaid and paid.*

- *Access to a combination of expert information resources, referral services, and counsel is also appreciated. In many cases, phone consultations or 24/7 expert hotlines are provided.*

- *In addition to the more obvious actions of providing time and flexibility and access to expert information, referrals, and counseling, truly nurturing a supportive workplace culture is critical to success. Visibly and actively promoting the idea that employee caregivers are supported by your company contributes to breaking down the negative stigma sometimes attached to caregiving.*

YOUR REVIEW PROCESS WILL SHOW YOU
EXACTLY WHERE YOUR COMPANY STANDS
IN TERMS OF PROVIDING
A RANGE OF EFFECTIVE SUPPORTS
FOR YOUR EMPLOYEE CAREGIVERS.

Regardless of whether your company has no supports in place, only a few, or already a good number, the review process will help you identify the gaps to be addressed in moving forward with developing a more robust employee caregiver support system.

Use your findings to draft out your provisional plan for the future, filling in obvious gaps

Going forward, the program and gaps to be addressed will also be informed by the survey results you'll be gauging. However, even before you have those results, there will no doubt be some glaring gaps you'll know need to be addressed.

After prioritizing the additional supports you believe are needed and will fit well within your company's ecosystem, go ahead and provisionally map out your plan for implementation, creating a strategy for years one, two, three – and beyond. You can change it as your various inputs from KPIs and employee surveys are available, and then the cycle begins again.

Additional ideas for filling the gaps are provided in the following section titled: Add Other Programs and Supports as Needed to Create a Virtuous Cycle.

Review and refine your plan at least a once a year.

A Built-in "Early Warning System" via Existing Manager-Employee Meetings

In addition to providing employee caregiver programs, it's important to identify emerging challenges with your employees as early in the process as possible so there's a fighting chance to manage the situation in the best way.

While the risk of being called upon to care for aging loved ones is greatest among female employees aged 40+ that risk is expanding quickly to include male employees, as well as younger-aged employees of both genders.

When managers are trained to address sensitive caregiving-related questions in bi-annual or annual performance appraisal meetings, these inputs can in turn lead to providing early support that lessens the negative impacts.

Attention to identifying employees who are also caregiving (and hence undergoing emotional, physical, and often also financial stressors) should therefore ideally be built into performance appraisal systems and other ongoing management systems – in the same manner that companies work to identify OTHER work and non-work stressors that negatively impact employees.

> ## Most Caregiving Situations Develop Unexpectedly, Pointing to the Need for Your Employees – and Your Company – to "Have a Plan"
>
> Most caregiving situations happen very quickly. It may well be because of a fall – the leading cause of injury and death for those aged 65+. Or it could be a cancer diagnosis or an Alzheimer's diagnosis.
>
> Because only about five percent of all families in the United States have had the kinds of discussions that lead to having a thorough and well-thought-out plan (including what will happen if and when caregiving support is required), most employees aged in their 40s, 50s and 60s are at high risk of having a sudden caregiving situation thrust upon them, throwing their lives into chaos.

Leverage key employee touchpoints

As part of reviewing what your company already offers, take this opportunity to identify key employee touchpoints through which you can communicate the programs you will be offering.

Employee touchpoints include but are not limited to:

- *HR department representative*
- *Onboarding interviews and programs*
- *Employee/Manager relationship*
- *Annual and/or semi-annual performance appraisal*

- *Work teams and other company colleagues (whether in-person or virtually)*

- *Training and development programs (internal and external)*

- *Employee surveys*

- *Company newsletter or other regular communications (digital or otherwise)*

- *Company Intranet (MSOffice with Teams/ Yammer/ SharePoint, etc.)*

- *Exit interviews*

These employee touchpoints are important to keep in mind, because as you'll see in a few pages, you're going to want to promote the availability of all you're doing as widely as possible among your total employee population as part of reinforcing the caring culture in your company.

Keep an eye out for KPIs

Another important aspect of your review is taking note of any KPIs you may already be using to monitor employee productivity and retention. Some of these existing KPIs can also be utilized (or expanded upon) to provide you with more data on employee caregiver-related impacts. Read on for more about establishing KPIs!

INDICATORS:
ESTABLISH KPIs

In the realm of HR metrics, most companies monitor employee activities, performance, and engagement, as well as the nuts-and-bolts of absenteeism, utilization of paid time off, and turnover.

The type and volume of metrics – and the regularity with which they are monitored – can vary greatly depending upon the company and its unique culture, ecosystem and policies. In addition, the extent to which these metrics are incorporated across departments so they can be synthesized into an overall viewpoint also varies.

> MOST EMPLOYERS DO NOT MEASURE THE IMPACT OF THEIR EMPLOYEES' CAREGIVING OBLIGATIONS ON THEIR ORGANIZATIONS… CLINGING TO THE PERCEPTION THAT THE COSTS ARE, AT WORST, MARGINAL. THIS SUPPORTS THEIR ASSUMPTION THAT TRACKING THEIR WORKFORCE'S CARE DEMOGRAPHICS AND MEASURING THE ASSOCIATED COSTS IS A SUPERFLUOUS EXERCISE. IN THE ABSENCE OF HARD DATA, FEW EMPLOYERS UNDERSTAND JUST HOW PROFOUND AN EFFECT CAREGIVING HAS ON COSTS AND PERFORMANCE IN TANGIBLE AND INTANGIBLE WAYS.

Source: The Caring Company, Harvard Business School, 2019

In consideration of company-to-company variability with metrics, as well as the need for companies to get started as soon as possible, the following suggestions are meant to serve as a starting point to help with your exploration of current and possible caregiver- and caregiving-related KPIs to suit your company's unique ecosystem.

Honing in on which metrics will work best for your company, you'll be focusing on:

- *Already monitored, standard KPIs for the entire employee population that can be adapted to your needs in monitoring employee caregivers, specifically.*

- *New monitoring of employee caregiver participation in various caregiver-centric. programs that are in place (and/or will be added).*

- *New ways of combining data for earlier problem detection and better crisis prevention.*

- *Additional outreach points to employees who may be struggling.*

- *Creating an overall Caregiving Crisis Cost Calculation scenario for your business. The resulting amount will represent a bare minimum, but it can serve as a benchmark against which to measure future caregiving crisis costs.*

The purposes of establishing KPIs, benchmarks, and ongoing monitoring are straightforward and necessary in order to:

1. Understand the negative impacts of at-home caregiving responsibilities on those who are employee caregivers (and to identify those at-risk as early as possible so appropriate support can be provided).

2. Understand the magnitude of the negative impact of turnover on the company – and improve retention through the addition of selected caregiver support programs.

3. Make an initial calculation of what caregiving-related losses cost your company on an annual basis. You will probably find that some of your inputs will change over time but getting a minimal estimate together initially can be eye opening.

What are Some Micro "Caregiver Cost-related Metrics" that Make Sense to Monitor?

The first and easiest metrics are those your company are already monitoring regularly – and then ensuring that you can see that data with specifics about employee caregivers.

At a micro level, many companies already monitor absentee-ism, as well as early signs of stress and pending burnout among the total employee population. Because studies show these areas as the top contributors to productivity losses related to employee caregivers, these KPIs also can serve as guideposts to managers that an employee is experiencing problems.

Example: Ideally, these two KPIs would be monitored so that when an employee appears to be distressed, based on their survey answers and attendance records, it would trigger notification to the manager. For instance, Jane Doe's answers to the recent Employee Engagement Survey, along with her absentee-ism record, could indicate that she may be experiencing difficulty in her personal life. As mentioned previously, the manager can then address the possible issue directly, in a one-to-one meeting with the employee.

What are Some Macro "Caregiver Cost-related Metrics" that Make Sense to Monitor?

At a macro level, overall retention and turnover is often used as a measure of employee engagement and satisfaction (i.e., how well does it stack up in your industry, and is it improving or declining?).

Understanding and managing retention and turnover have become even more important – and challenging – in the wake of the pressures brought on by pandemic-influenced workforce shifts.

Example: Even if an employee resigned due to caregiving responsibilities (and the company had not known about their challenges prior to that), this information would ideally be captured in the exit interview and communicated to the manager.

TRACKING AND UNDERSTANDING
WHEN (AND WHY) EMPLOYEE CAREGIVERS
LEAVE THE WORKFORCE IS CRITICAL,
SINCE STATISTICALLY
ONE-THIRD OF ALL WORKING CAREGIVERS
ULTIMATELY LEAVE THEIR JOBS
DUE TO THEIR
OVERWHELMING RESPONSIBILITIES AT HOME.

Further discussion with the employee – even after the official exit interview if necessary – could lead to a better understanding of how to prevent such situations from occurring in the future.

Additional possible KPIs to consider

Other KPIs to consider are those related to building in risk assessment and prevention going forward, such as tracking the various training programs and caregiver supports utilized by employee caregivers (and caregivers-to-be).

Each company will have its own ecosystem of employee wellbeing supports, including those obvious targets discussed earlier:

- *Health and wellness programs*

- *Coaching and counseling programs for stress management and burnout avoidance*

- *Financial planning and retirement planning programs*

- *Flexible time or remote/hybrid working programs*

- *'Working Mom' or 'working parent' programs' related allowance of paid or unpaid time off*

As such programs are re-purposed for the specific needs of employee caregivers, participation in such trainings is one easy metric, demonstrating employee uptake of the programs being offered. Even if uptake is less than expected, this is a point of invitation for a manager-employee one-on-one meeting to check in on the employee's wellbeing.

Once modules are added to address the needs of employee caregivers, it's good to scan those new offerings to determine whether there may be any KPI opportunities there (i.e., participant surveys pre- and post-training, etc.).

Read on for tips on how to calculate the cost of the Caregiving Crisis for your company.

How do you calculate the cost of the Caregiving Crisis for your company?

Again, in consideration of the wide variability in company cultures and monitoring systems, these suggestions are meant to serve as a starting point in developing your view of caregiver- and caregiving-related costs for your company ecosystem.

At first, the resulting amount will represent a bare minimum, and you will probably wish to revise some inputs over time. That's because you're building the measurement metrics while you are instituting improvements, making it a bit of a moving target.

However, going forward – and as the challenges related to the caregiving crisis expand – you will gain a clarified view and have a solid benchmark against which you can measure the progress of future caregiving crisis-related costs.

It's also important to keep in mind that you'll probably need two-to-three cycles of monitoring to assemble the metrics needed to gain an understanding of the true costs of the caregiving crisis to your company.

Four Easy Metrics to Consider		
Metric (Annualized Costs for …)	What to Ask	Guesstimating the Cost
Replacing # of employees who left due to caregiving	# of employees who've left in past year (due to caregiving specifically)	1.5 x salary of employees who left due to caregiving
Absentee-ism EAP program utilization Employee healthcare	Look at cost trends by employee segment (if possible, by age, gender, ethnicity, parent caregivers, caregivers of adults, etc.) Where are costs noticeably higher for one segment compared to others? These offer points of knowledge for further EAP improvement to reverse negative trends.	If you don't have the details for employee caregivers specifically (i.e., about why they left, why they were absent, whether or not they utilized EAP, or how much in healthcare costs), as a proxy just calculate the total for all employees as relevant, and then use 30% of that number – based on the fact that 30% of your workforce is actively caregiving for aging loved ones right now.

What are some key communications points in your company ecosystem where caregiver- and caregiving-related KPIs might be included?

- *Performance appraisals*

- *Semi-annual or annual employee surveys (engagement, climate, and/or culture surveys)*

- *Pulse surveys*

Again, leverage key employee touchpoints for KPI gathering, as needed

- *HR department representative*

- *Onboarding interviews*

- *Onboarding programs*

- *Employee/Manager relationship*

- *Annual and/or semi-annual performance appraisal*

- *Employee surveys*

Establishing KPIs is an important discussion. You'll want to take your company's current usage of KPIs for various measurements into account, especially in the HR area.

In AMI's (Aging Matters International's) deep-dive workshops, I walk you through some of the choices available to you and help you zero in on what will work best for your particular company ecosystem.

Check out our resources (many of which are free) related to establishing KPIs at

www.TheCaregivingCrisis.com

EMPLOYEES:
SURVEY YOUR EMPLOYEES
TO ENRICH YOUR UNDERSTANDING
OF THIS UNIQUE SEGMENT

Of course, as a market research professional, I'm opinionated on this matter. But why would you head into any situation – especially program innovation – without a good foundation of knowledge from a variety of inputs?

You've reviewed and repurposed existing programs and supports. You've made an initial plan for the next one-to-three years. You've established some KPIs with which to start.

Next, you're going to want to hear directly from your company's employee caregivers.

The Society of Human Resources Management (SHRM) Defines Three Common Survey Types

- *Employee opinion and satisfaction surveys, which measure employee views, attitudes and perceptions of the organization (i.e., "climate surveys").*

- *Employee culture surveys, which measure employee viewpoints and their alignment with that of the organization.*

- *Employee engagement surveys, which measure employees' commitment, motivation, sense of purpose and passion for their work and organization.*

Many companies conduct at least one of the above three types of surveys on an annual or semi-annual basis. In addition, so-called "pulse surveys" are popular during challenging times, as a way of checking in more frequently to monitor the negative impacts of stress on employee health and emotional wellbeing.

Utilize ongoing employee surveys

Explore the timing cycles and how and when you can give inputs to the questionnaire:

- *Review the questions asked.*

- *Add survey questions to address measurement of the KPIs you've identified.*

- *Add questions to identify your employee caregivers, to better understand their needs, and, to begin to predict future caregiving support needs for your company.*

In honing in on which questions will work best for supporting your company's monitoring objectives, you'll be focusing on:

- *Identifying existing questions that already offer insight (as long as the resulting data can be looked at "for employee caregivers" vs. "total employees")*

- *Modifying existing questions where appropriate (i.e., including "caregiving" as a multiple-choice selection)*

- *Adding new questions to:*

    ~ *Identify employees' positioning on the Caregiving Continuum*

    ~ *Explore which types of support they would most value*

    ~ *Identify at-risk employees as early as possible so appropriate support can be provided*

~ *Create deeper understanding of the negative impacts of at-home caregiving responsibilities on employees*

~ *Gauge the magnitude of the negative impact of turnover on the company*

Once you've gathered your first round of results and are able to identify your employee caregivers and their needs, you can begin to incorporate their inputs into your onward planning activities, adding supports that fulfill their specific requests. And the monitoring cycle begins again.

If your company does not have an employee survey in place, there are plenty of resources to help you get started. Please visit the www.TheCaregivingCrisis.com **for further resources, many of which are free.**

Augment Existing Online Surveys with Up-Close-and-Personal Discussions

There's no substitute for good, old-fashioned one-on-one interviews or discussions between managers and employees.

Caregiving is a sensitive and often personal area of discussion; it requires a similarly personal touch in terms of measurement and solutioning.

For this reason, it is best to incorporate qualitative research inputs into your decision-making via one-to-one discussion with your employee caregivers.

Ideally, these interviews should be conducted both before and following any online employee survey - before, so that inputs can be factored into the online survey questioning, and after, so you can drill down with employees who may be struggling.

ADD OTHER PROGRAMS
AND SUPPORTS AS NEEDED
TO CREATE
A VIRTUOUS CYCLE

Now that you're armed with greater clarity about your employee caregivers and their needs, clear KPIs, and an initial plan for repurposing and augmenting existing programs, it's time to address any remaining gaps with practical solutions for proactively managing the negative impacts of the caregiving crisis on your business – and providing much-needed support to your employee caregivers.

There is no one "right way" for companies to support employee caregivers; because company culture varies so greatly, each company must find its own unique way forward.

However, beyond the first three easy actions (i.e., reviewing and repurposing, establishing KPIs, and surveying your employee caregivers) there are many ways to move forward, including both internally and externally provided resources.

The solutions roadmap is rich and varied, with each component enhancing and reinforcing the positive impact of the others, including:

Training and skills-building to help meet employees' challenges in as balanced a manner as possible (including strategies for maintaining emotional, physical and financial health under duress) – and to give managers the tools they need to help employees with prevention and support.

Coaching, care coordination, and finding and securing resources to help employee caregivers get organized and find the best options for supporting their individualized caregiving situations… and to better cope through the most difficult times.

Content that supports and reinforces skills-building and coaching programs, as well as celebrates employee caregivers and all they do.

Technology that helps them organize, monitor, and manage their caregiving responsibilities with more ease.

Leadership in your company, by supporting the creation of Employee Resource Groups (ERGs) and other actions to demonstrate true commitment - and onward to your community, partnering with local non-profits as part of your corporate social responsibility outreach.

These additional supports and solutions can be expanded at any time in the process, staging them into your plan over several years if need be.

One way to expand the palette of caregiver-related supports your company offers is to outsource certain functions to specialty providers. Much like the outsourcing of HR automation (from core benefits administration to payroll functions), many aspects of what is needed to support your employee caregivers is already readily available.

Adding benefits – whether voluntary or included – should also be considered, especially as regards LTHC insurance options, because not taking LTHC costs into account can result in financial devastation for employees.

Many Typical Caregiver Support Programs Can be Outsourced (or Provided via a Partner) Directly to Your Employee Caregivers

You are only limited by your imagination! Even better, most of these programs are designed to require minimal support from your HR team, and include:

- *Lunch 'n Learn speakers on caregiving-related topics (for ERGs and wider employee audiences)*

- *Customizable content (articles, webinars, and podcasts for use in your employee publications and communications outreach)*

- *Semi-customized content (resource libraries)*

- *Manager training courses to make sure your managers' skills are up to speed when dealing with caregiving employees*

- *Employee training courses to quickly upskill your employees with the nuts and bolts of caregiving, as well as healing modalities for managing stress, grief, and relationships*

- *Care coordination and support during the caregiving experience, including researching and securing access to resources*

- *Digital platforms for coordinating care amongst multiple family members and professional caregiving (including scheduling, medical records, bill paying, and other important information)*

Add programs that go further than what is mandatory

Ten of my favorite ideas for going beyond the bare minimum when providing programs and supports to meet the needs of employee caregivers are:

1. Emergency backup care (nearly half of those companies surveyed provide this type of subsidized care, from 10~30 days a year).

2. Digital concierge services that can help support time-pressed caregivers of aging loved ones.

3. On-site support in the form of an aging-care consultant, who is responsible for coordinating access to eldercare benefits and resources for employees, including advising on care options and issues, providing referrals, and offering broad support.

4. On-site or off-site access to a care coordinator who works directly with employees and their families.

5. Exploration of employee caregiver needs on a continuous basis, as a way of gathering important inputs to designing their eldercare support programs (i.e., via confidential surveys, focus groups, and other information-gathering tools specifically among caregiving employees, as well as by incorporating a few questions about caregiving into existing engagement surveys, benefits open-enrollment processes, and other standard, regularly occurring HR-driven interactions with all employees).

6. Opportunity to use "flex time," which helps caregivers accommodate daytime doctor's appointments or other health/ medical-related appointments, including physical therapy.

7. "Time bank" that allows employees to donate their vacation or sick days to a coworker who is a caregiver.

8. Job-sharing experimentation to help make ends meet while fulfilling job responsibilities of caregiving employees.

9. Use of company intranet to create a "private community space" for those who are caregiving (some systems promote support groups and a community aspect, whereas others go so far as to provide employees with a secure and confidential space in which they can centralize their loved one's documents and share these with other family members, as a means of supporting smoother communications from afar).

10. Expanded paid-time leave and unpaid leave options.

These are all supports offered by companies that have moved beyond the foundational and continue to add programs that go even further in terms of meeting the needs of their employee caregivers.

For content solutions and for training and skills building (for both your managers and your employees), check out the resources and services offered by Aging Matters International (AMI), at www.TheCaregivingCrisis.com

AIM TO MAKE EMPLOYEE CAREGIVERS FEEL SEEN, ACKNOWLEDGED AND VALUED

One of the most important rewards of supporting your employee caregivers is that you will be moving one step closer to creating a caregiver-friendly workplace. What does this mean?

In short, it means that your company acknowledges its employee caregivers – through visible programs and informational content – with the result that these employees do not feel stigmatized because of their unavoidable off-work responsibilities.

Instead, they feel supported with both the preventive and real-time supports your company offers, including frontline manager training. Importantly, your employee caregivers feel valued and appreciated for what they are doing.

Having a robust caregiver support program in place and continuously working to deepen and strengthen it will go a long way toward improving retention. In addition, it will contribute to talent acquisition, because many employees are now expecting caregiver support benefits, especially Millennial-aged workers.

Another key takeaway from several studies is that it's not enough just to establish policies and programs that address your employee caregivers' needs. It's also important to communicate with employees who will someday soon become caregivers themselves, to help them get ahead of the curve.

Explore Ways of Recognizing Your Employee Caregivers and Creating a More Caregiver-Friendly Workplace

Five easy ways to get started are:

1. Provide information on caregiving benefits and how to access them as part of your employee onboarding process.

2. Address the overall topic of caregiving in employee publications and other communications (both digital and otherwise) through a series of articles to educate and inform your entire employee workforce about the challenges and support options.

3. Promote and explain your newly repurposed and other new programs designed to address the needs of employee caregivers, explaining who is eligible and how it works.

4. Feature your employee caregivers and their back stories (again, in employee publications and other employee communications).

5. Take advantage of November – designated as National Family Caregivers Month for more than 20 years – to rev up annual awareness-building, along with your year-round feed of news and feature stories.

In addition to demonstrating appreciation of your current employee caregivers, you'll be encouraging preparedness among your managers and non-caregiving employees by educating them about available programs and supports that your company offers.

Again, getting started and taking action in the right direction is the most important goal.

UNFORTUNATELY, EVEN AMONG COMPANIES
OFFERING A GENEROUS SLATE OF BENEFITS,
EMPLOYEE UNDERSTANDING
AND UTILIZATION OF THOSE BENEFITS
IS OFTEN LIMITED.

Proactive communication and internal marketing of caregiver-friendly workplace policies have two intangible and important payoffs:

First, they signal that the organization takes caregiving seriously and is compassionately committed to supporting its employees who are also caregiving.

Second, they help overcome employee caregiver concerns about whether managers might perceive them poorly if they take advantage of the program – and thereby improve program utilization rates.

For more ideas on utilizing employee communications channels as a means of educating and recognizing your employee caregivers - and of educating soon-to-be caregivers about preparedness - check out our resources at www.TheCaregivingCrisis.com

TAKE A LEADERSHIP ROLE
NOT ONLY WITH YOUR EMPLOYEES,
BUT ALSO IN YOUR COMMUNITY
AND WITH YOUR STAKEHOLDERS

Through training and role modeling, many organizations now strive to create a safe and caring cultural environment in which employees feel they can speak honestly with their supervisors and co-workers.

Extending this courtesy to encompass the special needs of employee caregivers seems to be an obvious imperative, considering these employees represent 30% of your workforce – and will represent an even greater proportion of your workforce going forward.

In fostering an environment that reinforces discussion around caregiving, it is important to ensure that visible top executives and frontline managers demonstrate their commitment to having a caregiver-friendly workplace.

Signals from the top demonstrate that leadership and the organization values taking care of aging loved ones.

NEARLY EVERY COMPANY INTERVIEWED
ACROSS SEVERAL STUDIES HAS MENTIONED
A SUPPORTIVE CULTURE
AS A KEY SUCCESS FACTOR.
HAVING PROGRESSIVE POLICIES ON THE BOOKS
REGARDING CAREGIVING FOR
AGING LOVED ONES
IS NOT ENOUGH.

Progressive companies with programs addressing the needs of employee caregivers are becoming more prevalent as the stressors related to the growing caregiving crisis deepen.

Reach beyond your own company for greater positive impact across your spheres of influence… with leadership and outreach to your stakeholder groups: current and potential customers, suppliers, legislators, and further to the communities in which your company operates, collaborating with non-profits and other organizations to provide caregiver supports.

Leadership can be demonstrated by sponsoring programs to educate selected disadvantaged audiences, or by sponsoring reports that highlight aspects of The Caregiving Crisis challenge. Both activities help build awareness and momentum, while supporting real caregivers who are struggling with very real challenges.

It doesn't have to cost an arm and leg to be innovative with employee caregiver support. It's actually rather straightforward and cost-effective to take a leadership position with your employees, your stakeholders, and your communities. There is so much common-sense yet high-impact work to be done!

I would love to help you and your company get started – or better leverage what you already have – in terms of employee caregiver support. Contact me for a free 30-minute consultation about how you can take a leadership role at your company. www.TheCaregivingCrisis.com

Let's also talk about how you can add your company's voice to the global discussion on workplace caregiving. If you'd like to be a guest on one of our podcasts or Clubhouse Rooms, just let me know: Debbie@TheCaregivingCrisis.com

REFERENCES

Articles and Reports: Landscape of Caregiving

Investors Guide to The Care Economy, 2021 report from Pivotal Ventures:
https://www.investin.care/#PVLI

Caregiving in the U.S. 2020, report from National Alliance for Caregiving and AARP, update of 23-year ongoing study
https://www.aarp.org/ppi/info-2020/caregiving-in-the-united-states.html

Family Caregiver Alliance, National Center on Caregiving
https://www.caregiver.org/caregiver-depression-silent-health-crisis

University of Michigan's Health and Retirement Study (HRS), Data on Aging in America since 1990?
http://hrsonline.isr.umich.edu/

National Center for Health Statistics (NCHS)
https://www.cdc.gov/nchs/fastats/older-american-health.htm
https://www.cdc.gov/ehrmeaningfuluse/National_Health_Care_Sur-veys.html

Center for Retirement Research at Boston College
http://crr.bc.edu/
http://crr.bc.edu/briefs/how-much-long-term-care-do-adult-children-provide/

Stanford Center on Longevity
https://longevity.stanford.edu/

The Center on Aging & Work at Boston College
https://www.bc.edu/research/agingandwork

Our World in Data, Oxford Martin Programme on Global Development at the University of Oxford
https://ourworldindata.org/life-expectancy

Life Expectancy in the USA, 1900-1998
http://www.demog.berkeley.edu/~andrew/1918/gure2.html

Articles and Reports: Caregivers in the Workplace

A New Generation of Family Caregivers Emerges During the Pandemic
https://www.newsecuritybeat.org/2021/07/generation-family-caregivers-emerges-pandemic/

Working Caregivers' Concerns and Desires in a Post-pandemic Workplace (AARP Report, 2021)
https://www.aarp.org/content/dam/aarp/research/surveys_statistics/ltc/2021/working-caregiver-survey.doi.10.26419-2Fres.00482.001.pdf

Few Employers Say their Current Wellbeing Programs Support Employees
https://www.willistowerswatson.com/en-US/News/2021/02/few-employers-say-their-current-wellbeing-and-caregiving-programs-effectively-support-employees

Research: Employer Perspective (Companies Expand Family-Friendly Policies, But Focus Favors Parents Over Caregivers)
https://www.spglobal.com/en/research-insights/featured/somethings-gotta-give

The Caring Company: How employers can help employees manage their caregiving responsibilities — while reducing costs and increasing productivity, report from Harvard Business School (2017 and 2019)
https://www.hbs.edu/managing-the-future-of-work/Documents/The_Caring_Company.pdf

Supporting Caregivers in the Workplace: Employer Benchmarking Survey (July, 2017), report from Northeast Business Group on Health (NEBGH)
https://nebgh.org/wp-content/uploads/2017/11/NEBGH-Caregiving_Practical-_Guide-FINAL.pdf

Supporting Working Caregivers: Case Studies of Promising Practices (2017), report from Respect a Caregiver's Time (ReACT)
https://respectcaregivers.org/wp-content/uploads/2017/05/AARP-ReAct-_MASTER-web.pdf

2017 Carers Report: Embracing the Critical Role of Caregivers Around the World, White Paper and Action Plan), Embracing Carers, Merck KGaA, Darmstadt, Germany
https://www.embracingcarers.com/content

Our Aging, Caring Nation: Why a U.S. Paid Leave Plan Must Provide More an Time to Care for New Children, a 2017 report issued by the National Partnership for Women & Families
https://www.nationalpartnership.org/our-work/resources/economic-justice/paid-leave/our-aging-caring-nation-why-a-us-paid-leave-plan-must-provide-more-than-time-to-care-for-new-children.pdf

2016 National Study of Employers (NSE), conducted by the Families and Work Institute (FWI), a project of SHRM (Society for Human Resource Management)
https://www.shrm.org/hr-today/trends-and-forecasting/research-and-surveys/Documents/National%20Study%20of%20Employers.pdf

ACKNOWLEDGEMENTS

As was true for my first book (*The Caregiving Journey: Information. Guidance. Inspiration.*), there is no proper way to express my profound gratitude to those who have helped me move this second book forward to completion.

As Mom passed in late 2008, I began brainstorming with Marcia Johnson in Tokyo about her work helping companies train employees on having difficult conversations with parents and loved ones.

Burning with a passion to help other caregivers, we organized a series of focus groups with corporate human resources (HR) managers in cooperation with the Japan Human Resources Society (JHRS) in Tokyo, with the objective of exploring the imperative to support employees in caring for their aging loved ones.

The results, published in a JHRS White Paper in October 2009 (*Workforce Management in Japan: A Look into the Aging Workforce and the Impending "Parent Care" Tsunami*) showed that both diversity and work life balance were considered more urgent than other top-of-mind concerns such as change management, talent management, and people development.

Marcia ended up moving to Shanghai in 2010 to help develop her husband's IT business, but before leaving Tokyo, she sold me the dot.com "Aging Matters International" (or AMI) - the umbrella under which I launched www.TheCaregivingJourney.com.

Fast forward to spring of 2016, when I officially launched AMI, and then 2018 when *The Caregiving Journey: Information. Guidance. Inspiration.* was published to support individual caregivers.

In further framing the conversation about workplace caregivers – and onward to leveraging offerings for corporations – I am grateful to:

- ***Deborah Harlow**, digital strategist and lifetime caregiver extraordinaire, who has worked with me tirelessly to establish AMI's newsletter, a private Facebook group, the Women Who Care podcast and annual Easy Self-care Challenge, and various tools to help individual caregivers, along with deep dives and webinars for corporate managers and employees.*

- ***Robin Weeks**, executive trainer and caregiver coach and advocate, my co-author in Fall of 2020 of our e-book titled* Employers Guide: Workplace Support for Family Caregivers (Assess. Support. Provide Benefits.), *in which we laid out many of the concepts that are foundational to creating a caregiver-friendly workplace.*

- *Fellow marketers **Jon Brody** and **Tanya Krim**, both of whom had recently obtained their degrees in gerontology. Together, in Spring 2021 we co-founded "Corporate Caregiver Camps" – a turnkey training and education solution for corporations, supported by the launch of our Caregiver Camps Podcast.*

- ***Linda Sherman** and **Dave Dlesk** (and **Marty Agather**) for their leadership of my two favorite Clubhouse Rooms*: Rethinking Aging/ Alliance to Create Age-friendly Products (formerly named Products for 50+) *and* MedStartr's Preventive Care for Aging Adults. *They have graciously allowed me to bring the important workplace caregiver topic into their wider dialogues. The Rethinking Aging Club also sponsors the room* Shifting the Culture of

Caregiving, *which I co-host with* **Christina Keys** *of Caregiving.com. My thanks to Christina, too!*

- **Doug Bruhnke** *and* **Cesar Trebanco** *of the Global Chamber – along with* **Steve Sowerby** *and* **Dave McCaughan** *of the Consumer Healthcare Training Academy, and also* **John David Spade** *of Always United (an affinity group with the United Way, the Midlands) – also generously provided fora for discussing these important issues.*

In addition, I'm very appreciative of the inputs from over 100 interviews with C-suite and HR leaders.

Once again, my publisher and book coach, **Steph Ritz**, came through for me with her usual excellent guidance. Her talents as a storyteller and coach – not to mention as a business strategist – have made her an invaluable advisor to me. My thanks also go to my writing partner, creativity muse **Vivian Geffen**, with whom I met online to write on three mornings a week throughout the summer!

My significant other, **Bob**, has steadfastly supported me through the stages one must go through with any big project. The Central Texas Hill Country (my home and refuge from big city life in Tokyo – and during the prolonged pandemic), has continued to demonstrate its healing energy.

My cousin **Kay McDonald** — a pioneer in social entrepreneuring — has been a constant source of inspiration, especially for "all things digital." Kay founded Phoenix, Arizona-based Charity Charms back in 2004, a company specializing in strategic awareness-building that has raised millions for non-profit organizations worldwide.

Kay, along with friends **Bonnie, Catherine, Alison and Alison** (you know who you are!), **Deb**, and my sisters **Marcia** and **Sandy** have provided excellent ears, ideas and counsel on a regular basis.

I'd also like to recognize illustrator **Adrienne Baker** for her wonderful renditions of my "napkin sketches" – bravo! And a big thank you to the peeps at Little Bird Marketing for their help with my social media!

A special shout out goes to my childhood friend, **Beth Reiber** (the original inspiration for my moving to Japan) ... who expertly commandeered the line edit of the book.

Other friends have been spared the frequency and volume of listening but have nonetheless served as wonderful sounding boards, giving me advice and moral support along the way: **Betsey, Nancy Ann, Sue Ann** and **Chick**.

Finally, I would like to thank my Tokyo-based business partner, **Dominic Carter**, for his continued patience with my caregiving journey.